Disney

RALPH BREAKS THE INTERNET

Level 6

Re-told by: Vessela Gasper
Series Editor: Rachel Wilson

T0383563

Contents

In This Book — iii

Before You Read — iv

Chapter 1: Sugar Rush Breaks Down — 1

Chapter 2: Ralph Has a Plan — 6

Chapter 3: KnowsMore Has the Answer — 9

Chapter 4: Shank and Slaughter Race — 12

Chapter 5: Ralph's Videos Go Viral — 16

Chapter 6: Good News, Bad News — 19

Chapter 7: The Virus Takes Over — 23

Chapter 8: Ralph's Fight — 29

Chapter 9: Best of Friends — 33

After You Read — 37

Glossary — 38

Play: Connect with the World! — 40

Global Citizenship: Online School Communities — 41

Find Out: What is a computer virus? — 42

Phonics — 44

In This Book

Wreck-It Ralph

The Bad Guy in the video game *Fix-It Felix Jr.*

Vanellope von Schweetz

The best racer in the video game *Sugar Rush*

KnowsMore

A character who helps people find things on the Internet

Spamley

A character with a pop-up message looking for people who want to get rich

Shank

A racer in the video game *Slaughter Race*

Yesss

A character from a video-sharing website

Before You Read

Introduction

Ralph and his best friend Vanellope live happily in Mr. Litwak's Arcade. Every day after work, they meet with friends to play games and tell jokes. But after many years of racing in *Sugar Rush*, Vanellope is bored and wants to do something more exciting. Ralph surprises her with a new track, but her steering wheel gets broken. They go on a dangerous adventure to look for a new one. They meet new characters and discover a new world, full of exciting things. Will they find a steering wheel to save the video game? Will they still be friends?

Activities

1 Look at the title and the pictures on pages 1–4. Where do you think Ralph and Vanellope work?

1 inside a computer **3** in a store **5** nowhere

2 in the Internet **4** in video games

2 What do you think? Which of these sentences are NOT main ideas in the story?

1 Video games are bad for children.

2 Good friends always help each other.

3 You need to be wise and careful when you use the Internet.

4 Only boys can be fast racers.

1 Sugar Rush Breaks Down

Wreck-It Ralph and Vanellope von Schweetz were best friends. They did everything together! They both worked in Mr. Litwak's Family Fun Center and Arcade. Ralph was the Bad Guy in a popular video game, *Fix-It Felix Jr.*, and Vanellope was the best racer in another game, *Sugar Rush*.

Every day after work, Ralph and Vanellope met in Game Central Station, the place where all the machines joined together. There, they spent time talking, playing games, and telling jokes. They were happy and life was good.

But one day, on their way to work, they heard something. Someone said there was a new game. They decided to go and see it. They watched the game's name light up: *Wi-Fi*. But it wasn't a game! It connected the Arcade to the Internet. It was something new, something different.

Vanellope wasn't happy about this Wi-Fi thing. She wanted a new racing game—faster and more exciting. She loved *Sugar Rush*, but after so many years racing on the same tracks, the game wasn't interesting enough or hard enough for her.

Ralph had an idea.

Ralph went inside *Sugar Rush* and made a new track for his friend.
It was filled with dangerous jumps.

"She's gonna love this!" thought Ralph.

Vanellope was winning the game until something happened.
The girl playing the game in the Arcade turned the steering wheel
really hard. It broke in her hands!

Inside the game, Vanellope couldn't steer her car and crashed!
Ralph was worried, "Oh man, I'm so sorry. Are you okay?"

"That was so much fun!" cried Vanellope. She thought it was an
amazing track. "Thank you, thank you, thank you!"

Mr. Litwak tried to fix the steering wheel, but he couldn't.
The girl found another one on a website called eBay. But it was
too expensive.

"That's more than this game makes in a year! I hate to do it,
but I have to sell *Sugar Rush* for parts.' he said.

Ralph heard him and told the others. "Litwak's gonna unplug
your game! Go! Run, run, run!" he shouted.

Mr. Litwak reached for the plug. All the characters in *Sugar Rush*
ran toward Game Central Station as fast as they could.

Vanellope went home with Ralph. She didn't have a game and she didn't have a home. "What am I gonna do all day?" she said sadly.

Ralph tried to make her feel better. "That's the best part. You sleep in every day. You do no work."

"But I loved my game! If I'm not a racer," said Vanellope, "who *am* I?"

"Well, you're my best friend!" Ralph said.

Vanellope didn't want to hurt his feelings, but life without the racing track sounded boring. She told him she just needed to be alone, and walked away.

[2] Ralph Has a Plan

Later that evening, Ralph had an idea. He went to find Vanellope.

"We're going to the Internet!" he told his friend.

"What?!" Vanellope didn't understand.

Ralph explained his plan: "We go to the Internet, find eBay, get the steering wheel, and send it to Mr. Litwak. He'll fix your game. Everything goes back to the way it was. BOOM!" he said proudly.

Vanellope loved the idea. She was so excited! The two friends ran toward Game Central Station.

Ralph and Vanellope went inside the Wi-Fi plug. The first stop was a large, empty space. Vanellope thought they were already in the Internet. It seemed boring …

Just then, Mr. Litwak logged on to the Internet.

"Look!" said Vanellope pointing at a small character, who looked like Mr. Litwak. He was moving inside the Wi-Fi plug. "Come on, Ralph, let's follow him."

"Whoa! Cool!" shouted Vanellope. They were both flying into the Internet at top speed. "Ralph! Isn't this great?!"

"No, it is *not*!" he replied. Ralph couldn't breathe.

The friends went fast. It was a wild race, and Vanellope was excited. She loved every second of it.

Finally, they arrived at the center of the Internet. It was amazing—the place was so big, and so different than Litwak's Arcade.

"We are in the Internet! C'mon, Ralph!" said Vanellope. "Whoa. This is the most beautiful thing I've ever seen." She couldn't wait to start exploring.

"Yeah, it's really something," Ralph replied.

"But it's too big. It goes on and on. How are we ever gonna find eBay out there?" asked Vanellope.

"It's okay. Not to worry. I'm sure there's someone who could tell us the way …," said Ralph.

3 | KnowsMore Has the Answer

Ralph could see a little character wearing big, round glasses and
a funny hat. He was standing behind a desk. "Maybe he could help us,"
he told Vanellope. The two friends walked over to him.

"Oh, hello, Sir. Welcome to the Search Bar. What can KnowsMore
help you find today?" the little man asked. He seemed very friendly.

"Um …" First Ralph tried to explain, but it didn't help.

Then Vanellope tried. "eBay—*Sugar Rush*—steering wheel!"
she said quickly.

KnowsMore knew what to look for, and immediately found the
Sugar Rush steering wheel.

Ralph and Vanellope went off to eBay at top speed. It was a busy place filled with characters and pop-up messages. Ralph looked left and right—they were all talking at once, and they were talking to him!

"You've won!" said one pop-up.

"Really?" Ralph was amazed.

"Wanna get rich playing video games? Click here to find out how," said another.

"That sounds interesting," Ralph pointed to the message.

Vanellope pulled him away. There was no time to look around. They had to hurry to get the steering wheel.

Inside eBay, people were calling out numbers. Vanellope saw the steering wheel.

"Oh, there it is! I see it. Whoa, someone else is trying to win it. Hurry, let's go."

"We have two seventy-five," a man said. "Do I hear three?"

"Three!" Ralph called out.

"One thousand!" said Vanellope.

Ralph and Vanellope kept going. They thought they had to call out the biggest number to win the steering wheel.

"Sold!" said the man. "For twenty-seven thousand and one!" The two friends felt great. Then they realized that they had to find twenty-seven thousand and one dollars in 24 hours to pay for it!

Shank and Slaughter Race

The two friends went back to the man with the pop-up message. "Can you please tell us how to get rich playing video games?" they asked.

His name was Spamley and he was happy to help. He showed them some things in video games. They could find them and win money. Spamley asked them if forty thousand dollars was enough. "It's more than enough." Ralph was excited.

Spamley explained that they needed to bring him Shank's car. It was from a dangerous game called *Slaughter Race*. "This kid's the best racer in the whole world! We'll get you the car, no problem!" Ralph said proudly.

Vanellope and Ralph went to the game. They saw two characters trying to steal Shank's car. But Shank and her team kicked them out of the game. *Slaughter Race* made Ralph nervous, but Vanellope loved it, "This game is cool!" She had an idea. She asked Ralph to talk to Shank and her team.

"I'm here from the, ah, Department of Noise?" Ralph started talking to them.

No one was looking at the car. Before Shank could see her, Vanellope quickly climbed inside her car. She started the car, picked up Ralph, and drove away. But Shank climbed into another car and raced after them.

"I believe you have something of mine!" Shank shouted, as she raced after them.

"Yeah, come and get it!" Vanellope shouted back.

"Oof, this girl can drive!" thought Shank.

Vanellope tried her best, racing off the track through some burning buses. But Shank was fast, and Vanellope couldn't escape.

"You thought you could just steal my car?" Shank was angry. Ralph tried to explain. He told Shank that they needed her car to win some money. They needed to save Vanellope's racing game.

Ralph was surprised when Shank said she wanted to help. But she didn't want to give them her car. Suddenly, one of her friends started shooting a video of Ralph. He told Ralph to do something crazy. Ralph and Vanellope didn't understand.

Shank explained that anyone could make money by putting crazy videos on the Internet. Her friend Yesss could help them. "Tell her I sent you."

"Wow, that's really nice of you," replied Vanellope.

Shank climbed into her car. She told Vanellope she could come back and race her again. Vanellope smiled. She really liked *Slaughter Race*. It was more exciting than *Sugar Rush*.

5 Ralph's Videos Go Viral

Vanellope and Ralph went to meet Yesss, who worked at a very popular, video-sharing website. It was called BuzzzTube. At first, Yesss didn't want to let them in. Then she realized that Ralph's video had a lot of *hearts*. She put it on her website and told Ralph that he was becoming famous.

Seconds later, Ralph was all over the Internet. "Well, Wreck-It Ralph, you are popular! And these are all for you. Heart, heart, heart, heart, heart, heart, heart!" said Yesss.

Vanellope didn't understand. "Shank said that viral videos can make *real* money …" she told Yesss. "Oh, hearts *are* money," Yesss explained.

A few seconds later, Ralph noticed that he didn't have many hearts. He needed to make more videos very quickly. He decided to fill BuzzzTube with his crazy videos.

Yesss helped him to make more videos. Ralph enjoyed doing crazy things—eating a hot pepper, burning his food, dancing, screaming, jumping, hitting things …

Yesss said they had enough videos. Now they needed as many hearts as possible to save the game.

Ralph loved seeing the number of hearts go up and up. The plan was working and he felt great.

Yesss was putting the last video on her website when Ralph went inside another room. The walls were full of messages. He started reading them.

"So stupid"

"Ralph is THE WORST!"

"I HATE HIM."

"He's SO fat and ugly."

Ralph felt terrible. He realized people were giving him hearts because they were laughing at him. They even hated him!

"Oh, Ralph, this is the first thing you have to learn about the Internet," said Yesss. "Do not read the comments. Look, this place can show the worst in some people."

"It's fine," he told Yesss. "As long as Vanellope likes me, I don't need anyone else."

Good News, Bad News

Ralph had all the money they needed to fix *Sugar Rush*. He hurried back to eBay. On his way, he called Vanellope with the good news.

"We did it! We got the money!" shouted Ralph.

"No way! Ralph, that's great," replied Vanellope.

"Meet me in five minutes?" he asked.

"Okay. I'll see you soon," she answered.

"We're going home!" Ralph replied.

He didn't know that she was meeting Shank. After Vanellope spoke to Ralph, she realized that she wasn't happy. She didn't want to leave the Internet. She liked *Slaughter Race* so much. It was new, different, and exciting.

Ralph left eBay and video-called Vanellope using something called BuzzzFace. Her phone turned on and fell on the seat next to her. Ralph saw that she was with Shank. Vanellope couldn't hear him, but he could hear them talking.

"The second I walked into this game, it felt like home," Vanellope told Shank. "It's my dream. You never know what's going to happen next. Back home, I know exactly what's gonna happen. That's because Ralph's dream is to do the same thing every day," she explained.

"Best friends don't have to have the same dreams," Shank replied.

"I can't go home. I just can't," said Vanellope.

Ralph felt so alone. He couldn't believe what Vanellope said to Shank. He worried that he would lose his best friend.

He told Spamley he needed to get her out of *Slaughter Race* immediately. He couldn't let her stay in a game that was bad for her. Spamley told Ralph to be careful and not to get angry.

"Then how do I make her leave, huh?" replied Ralph. "She thinks it's so cool and exciting in there …"

Suddenly, Ralph had an idea. "Wait—you know about computer viruses, right?" Perhaps a virus could make the game slow and boring …

Spamley took Ralph to a place called the Dark Net. There, they met Double Dan, Spamley's friend.

"Double Dan! How are things?" said Spamley.

"Now, what are you doing here?" Double Dan said, turning to look at Ralph.

Ralph explained why he was there. He wanted Double Dan to give him a virus that could slow down the *Slaughter Race* game. The virus was inside a box. Double Dan showed it to Ralph. He said, "All you have to do is make sure the virus stays in *Slaughter Race*."

Later, Ralph hid the box inside *Slaughter Race*.

7 The Virus Takes Over

Vanellope was waiting to start her first race inside *Slaughter Race*. "Hey, don't be nervous. You're gonna be great," said Shank. But Vanellope was worrying about Ralph. She was afraid to tell him her plans. She didn't want to lose him, and she didn't want to hurt him.

"Look, all friendships change, and the good ones—they get stronger because of it," said Shank.

"Okay," replied Vanellope.

"All right. Let's race!" called Shank.

Vanellope started her car, but she didn't notice the virus coming out. It began to work immediately.

Soon, the whole game began to break up. A piece of a building crashed on top of Vanellope's car. "Oh, no …!" screamed Vanellope. She couldn't move. Everything went dark.

Ralph was watching the game from the outside. He saw that the buildings were falling down. The whole game was crashing!

Ralph quickly made a hole and went inside *Slaughter Race*. It was really dangerous. He pulled his friend from the broken car and carried her outside the game.

"Come on, Vanellope. Wake up," he said. "I can't live without you."

Vanellope opened her eyes and saw Ralph. He looked worried. She felt bad. She thought the game broke because of her stupid dreams. Then it was Ralph's turn to feel bad, so he told her about the virus.

"A virus? You did this?" Vanellope was really angry.

He also said that he knew about her conversation with Shank. He knew that she didn't want to go back to *Sugar Rush*.

Vanellope didn't want to listen to him. She didn't want to spend another second with him. She threw Ralph's Hero Medal away. Then she turned and ran away.

"No, Vanellope, don't leave me now. What have I done ...?" Ralph said to himself. He didn't notice the virus escaping from the *Slaughter Race* game. Soon, it was attacking the whole Internet.

Ralph went to look for his Hero Medal. When he found it, it was broken in two pieces.

Then he heard a loud sound behind him. He turned around and saw his own face. "Oh, no," said Ralph. "What did I do?" There were thousands of characters and they all looked like Ralph. Then the Internet started to crash.

Vanellope was back at the center of the Internet, the place where
they first arrived. Suddenly, she saw Ralph.

"What's your problem, Ralph? I told you not to follow me!"
she shouted at him. But this wasn't her friend, it was the virus Ralph.

He was excited to see her. He said, "Friend!" and ran toward her.
Other virus Ralphs followed him and they all shouted, "Friend!"

Vanellope was scared. She tried to hide behind a corner, but there
were more of them. She started to run faster.

Vanellope ran to KnowsMore. She told him that a lot of Ralphs were following her.

"Well, isn't that interesting!" he replied. As the Ralphs got closer, they both tried to hide from them.

Then the real Ralph arrived. "It's me! It's the real me!" he shouted. "I'm so glad you're okay, I followed those things here. I think they're looking for you, Vanellope!"

KnowsMore explained what was happening. The virus was growing because Ralph was afraid of losing his best friend. They needed to get all the Ralphs to the Antivirus District. The software there would delete them.

8 Ralph's Fight

Ralph had an idea. He knew that the Ralphs would follow Vanellope. She could lead them to the gate of the Antivirus District. Everyone agreed that it was a good idea. They just needed someone with a fast car ... Vanellope thought of Yesss from BuzzzTube.

Yesss arrived very quickly. Ralph put his head through the car roof. Vanellope climbed in the seat next to Yesss.

"I can't believe he did this ...," she started saying to Yesss.

"But he also made those crazy videos to help you," Yesss replied. It was true. Ralph made a mistake, but he also helped her.

Yesss drove her car toward the Antivirus District. Vanellope stood on the car roof and shouted, "It's me, your best friend in the whole wide world, who you can't live without!"

Thousands of virus Ralphs began to follow her. But then they became a big wave, which sent Yesss' car through the window of a tall building. The car crashed!

Everyone was okay, but not for long. They watched as the Ralphs now changed into something even worse—one, big virus Ralph! It was horrible!

The big virus Ralph picked up Vanellope and carried her to the top of a tall building. The real Ralph jumped after them. "Hey! Get back here! You put her down!"

Vanellope was able to escape with Ralph's help. But then the virus Ralph caught the real Ralph! He held him very tightly. Ralph was in real pain.

Vanellope shouted at the big Ralph, "Stop it! You're gonna kill my best friend! Put him down and take me. I know that's what you want," continued Vanellope.

But then the real Ralph said, "No, that's not what I want."

The big virus Ralph was listening closely. "It's not right to hold a friend back from her dreams. You don't own her. That's not how friendship works. You need to let her go," said Ralph. Then he turned to Vanellope, "And we're gonna be okay, right?"

"Of course we are," she replied. "Always!"

Ralph stopped being afraid of losing his friend. "I feel good about this," he said.

Suddenly, the big Ralph disappeared. Soon, all the virus Ralphs were gone as well. The Internet was okay again!

9 Best of Friends

Ralph sat with Vanellope. It was almost her time to race in *Slaughter Race*.

"I've just realized—there's no day or night here. Everything's always on," said Ralph.

"That's smart of you to notice," replied Vanellope.

"Other than KnowsMore, I'm probably the smartest person on the Internet," said Ralph.

"Yeah," Vanellope laughed.

Ralph was sad to say goodbye to his best friend. But he was also happy for her.

"It's gonna be great! You'll be fine. You've found your dream game!" he told her.

"Oh, before you go, I wanted to give you this." Ralph gave her one half of his broken Hero Medal.

"Oh, I'm so sorry I broke it …," said Vanellope.

Ralph smiled. "No, no, it's okay. Now we can both have a half. See?" He pulled out his half, which was around his neck.

Vanellope jumped into his arms. "I love you so much. I'm really gonna miss you."

"I'm gonna miss you, too," said Ralph. "Go on, get outta here. The world's waiting for you!"

Ralph watched his best friend go into her new game and he felt sad.

Then, Ralph went back home to Mr. Litwak's Arcade. Ralph and Vanellope used BuzzzFace to talk at night. Ralph gave Vanellope all the news.

"I'll be honest, it still feels strange here without you," he said. "I mean, a lot has changed. Yes, we got the steering wheel and saved *Sugar Rush*, but it's never really gonna feel the same …," he continued. "For a start, the *Sugar Rush* racers are nicer to each other!"

He told Vanellope how the characters cared more about friendship than winning the race, these days.

"I joined the book club," Ralph told his friend. "Oh, and we do this thing every Friday night—we all go to a different game to eat, talk, and have fun. It was my turn this week. I burned the food ..."

Vanellope loved his funny stories. Ralph was planning to visit her in two months. But she wished they could see each other sooner.

It was dawn—nearly time to go to work. "Talk next week," said Vanellope.

Ralph and Vanellope didn't spend every day together, but they were still the very best of friends.

After You Read

1 **Put the story into the correct order.**

a A virus attacks *Slaughter Race*.

b Ralph and Vanellope go inside the Internet.

c The *Sugar Rush* steering wheel breaks.

d Ralph's videos go viral.

e Mr. Litwak unplugs *Sugar Rush*.

f Ralph buys the steering wheel from eBay.

g Ralph saves the Internet.

2 **Read through the story quickly to find this information:**

1 KnowsMore told Ralph and Vanellope where to buy a …

2 To get the steering wheel, Ralph and Vanellope paid …

3 Yesss worked at a popular video-sharing website called …

4 For his crazy videos, Ralph got lots of …

5 Vanellope started the *Slaughter Race*, but didn't see the …

6 Before Ralph said goodbye to Vanellope, he gave her one half of his …

3 **Answer the questions. What do you think? Tell a friend.**

1 Why did Ralph want to get a new steering wheel?

2 Why didn't Ralph like Shank?

3 Why did Vanellope want to stay in *Slaughter Race*?

4 Why did Ralph put the virus in *Slaughter Race*?

5 How has Ralph changed by the end of the story?

Glossary

character (*noun*) a person or a living thing in a book, play, movie, video game, etc.

click past tense **clicked** (*verb*) to choose something on a computer to make the computer do something; *Click here to find out how.*

comment (*noun*) something you say or write that shows what you think of it.

connect past tense **connected** (*verb*) to join two or more things together; *It connected the Arcade to the Internet.*

crash past tense **crashed** (*verb*) 1. [car, etc.] to have an accident by hitting something else; *A piece of a building crashed on top of Vanellope's car.* 2. [computer] to break; *Then the Internet started to crash.*

crazy (*adj.*) wild, strange, or not sensible

dawn (*noun*) the very beginning of the day, when light first appears

delete past tense **deleted** (*verb*) to take away information from a computer; *The software there would delete them.*

fix past tense **fixed** (*verb*) to mend something when it is broken; *Mr. Litwak tried to fix the steering wheel, but he couldn't.*

friendship (*noun*) feelings between friends

log on (*verb*) past tense **logged on** to start using a computer by writing your password; *Just then, Mr. Litwak logged on to the Internet.*

plug in /unplug past tense **plugged in / unplugged** (*verb*) to connect something to the electricity so that it can work; *Litwak's gonna unplug your game!*

pop-up (*noun*) a computer window, that suddenly appears, with information selling you something

software (*noun*) instructions that tell a computer how to do a job

steering wheel (*noun*) a wheel that you turn to make a car go forward, turn left, or right

track (*noun*) a path that people or cars can move along or drive on

video (*noun*) a short movie, that you can make using a camera or a phone, that people watch on the Internet

virus (*noun*) software that is secretly put into a computer to delete or steal information

viral (*adj.*) when a lot of people on the Internet share a video, picture, or message in a short time

website (*noun*) a place on the Internet where you can find information about something

Play: Connect with the World!

Scene 1:

In his Family Fun Center, Mr. Litwak is plugging something in. Ralph, Vanellope, and other characters are watching him from inside Game Central Station.

RALPH: It says Wi-Fi … What is it?

SONIC: The Internet! I heard it's amazing!

SURGE PROTECTOR: Oh, no it's not! The Internet is new and different. We should be afraid of it! Get back to work and keep away.

RALPH: [quietly to Vanellope] Let's go to the Internet and find out for ourselves.

Scene 2:

Later, Ralph and Vanellope go inside the Internet and look around.

RALPH: [looking at eBay] Wow! We can buy things from anywhere!

KNOWSMORE: [popping up] Hi, what do you want to know? Just ask me!

VANELLOPE: We can learn about anything and everything!

RALPH: [looking at sign] Look! It says, "Join our community."

VANELLOPE: We can make friends from all around the world!

Scene 3:

Suddenly there are a lot of pop-ups.

SPAM 1: Hey you! Just click here to get $10,000!

SPAM 2: Hey! Give me your password and win a car!

RALPH: That sounds great!

VANELLOPE: No! It's not true.

RALPH: Maybe Surge Protector was right about the Internet …

VANELLOPE: We just have to be careful. The Internet's amazing. If we're careful, we can connect with the world!

Global Citizenship

Online School Communities

Learning about the world is important. It's also important to learn *with* the world. The Internet makes this possible.

An organization called iEARN (International Education and Resource Network) connects millions of students from more than 140 countries. Schools work together on global learning projects. Students meet in online forum spaces to talk about their projects.

One project is called the *Cultural Exchange Package*. Two schools from different countries send each other a box of things from their country.

First, students meet online to learn about each other's school, town, and country. Then, they decide what things to send to the other school. They find the things, write about them, and send the box. Finally, after each school receives the box, they meet in the online forum and talk about the things in the box.

What is a computer virus?

It's difficult to imagine a world without the Internet. We use the Internet to send information quickly between computers. Computers use software. The software tells the computer to send a message, play a video game, or do something else.

Computer engineers usually write software that's helpful. But there are other people who write software to make computers sick. That's where computer viruses come from. One of the first computer viruses was called The Creeper. It sent out a message saying, *I'm the creeper, catch me if you can.*

Antivirus software helps to keep personal information safe.

When the virus goes inside a computer, it starts to make copies of itself over and over. It can delete information, make your computer crash, or attack email addresses. Other people start receiving emails with the virus. Then the bad software infects many more computers.

Emails often have links to websites infected by viruses. They ask people to click on the links or reply with their personal information, such as passwords or addresses. This is called "phishing."

How to stop phishing:

- Don't open messages from names you don't know
- Don't click on links from names you don't know
- Don't share your personal information
- Use a strong password with a mix of letters and numbers
- Change your password often
- Use antivirus software

infect (*verb*) to make something or someone sick
password (*noun*) a secret group of letters or numbers
personal (*adj.*) belonging to one person

Phonics

Say the sounds. Read the words.

al

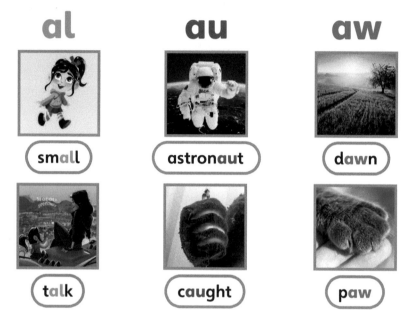

small

talk

au

astronaut

caught

aw

dawn

paw

Read, then say the rhyme to a friend.

Ralph was very tall, Vanellope was small.
Best friends for ever, they talked until the dawn.

Vanellope loved a place, a game called *Slaughter Race*.
When Ralph made a call, he saw it on her face.

Then buildings began to fall, so Ralph broke the wall!
And the virus caught his friend. How would the story end?